746

D1338414

THE VICTORIA AND ALBERT COLOUR BOOKS

FIRST PUBLISHED IN GREAT BRITAIN BY
WEBB & BOWER (PUBLISHERS) LIMITED
9 COLLETON CRESCENT, EXETER, DEVON EX2 4BY
AND MICHAEL JOSEPH LIMITED, 27 WRIGHTS LANE, LONDON W8 5TZ
IN ASSOCIATION WITH THE VICTORIA AND ALBERT MUSEUM, LONDON

BOOK, COVER AND SLIP CASE DESIGN BY CARROLL, DEMPSEY & THIRKELL LIMITED

BRITISH LIBRARY CATALOGUING IN PUBLICATION DATA
HINCHCLIFFE, FRANCES
THIRTIES FLORAL FABRICS - (THE VICTORIA AND ALBERT COLOUR BOOKS)
1. TEXTILE DESIGN - HISTORY - 20th CENTURY
I. TITLE
746 NK9500

ISBN 0-86350-214-8

PRODUCTION BY FACER PUBLISHING
COLOUR REPRODUCTION BY PENINSULAR REPRO SERVICE, EXETER
TYPESET IN GREAT BRITAIN BY OPTIC

PRINTED AND BOUND IN HONG KONG BY
MANDARIN OFFSET

THE VICTORIA AND ALBERT COLOUR BOOKS

THIRTIES
FLORAL FABRICS

INTRODUCTION BY
FRANCES HINCHCLIFFE

WEBB & BOWER
MICHAEL JOSEPH
MCMLXXXVIII

 IN THE 1930s it was considered 'the height of chic' to attend a formal garden party in a soft floating dress bedecked with a pattern of summer blooms, worn under a large shady straw 'sailor' hat. It was equally modish to simply allow a frock, scattered with dainty flower heads, to peep demurely from beneath a winter coat. Floral printed fabrics held a prominent place in every smart woman's wardrobe, whether she could afford to be dressed by a Parisian couturier or had to rely on a paper pattern and her own home dressmaking skills.

The long, slim lines of the 1930s silhouette were achieved by cutting material on the cross so that it would shape and mould to the body. Resulting in complex piecing and intricate diagonal seaming, this demanded small scale patterns and designs without obvious directions or repeats. Motifs floating on a plain ground worked admirably, such as detached heads of garden pinks *(plate 25)* or a shower of seedpods gently drifting to the ground *(plate 4)*. Navy, black and brown background colours were perennially in vogue. Designs which covered the whole surface were also successful; papery, scarlet poppies contrasted with black and white hard-edge ellipses *(plate 5)*, a carpet of daisies and shadowy leaves set against a random array of spots *(plate 2)*, or a profusion of blooms nestling among foliage *(plate 22)*.

Field flowers were as popular as the cultivated garden varieties. 'Comin' through the Rye' designs *(plates 15 and 17)* evoke the breeze rippling through a meadow or cornfield on a summer's day. Loose bunches of poppies, daisies and grasses lend an air of grace and movement, echoing the fluidity and sup-pleness of the fabrics on which they are printed – crêpe de Chines, satins, georgettes, chiffons and voiles. These silks, rayons and fine cottons are pliable and, unlike stiffer cloths, can be draped, ruched or frilled as desired. They can be gathered and puffed to make a sleeve, left unrestrained to float as a cape around the shoulders, or added as a finishing touch of delicate fluttery bows.

Silk retailed at about twice the price of its man-made substitute, rayon. In 1935 a yard of D. Marshall & Co. Ltd's printed rayon 'Crêpe Santos' (35-36 inches wide) could be purchased for just 3/11 d (approximately 20 pence). At the upper end of the market the London department store Harvey Nichols advertised 'New! Floral Matt Crêpe for summer gowns ... a lovely and inexpensive solution to summer dress problems! The fascinating matt

 crêpe is made entirely of fine rayon, and is a little heavier than a soft crêpe de Chine – just right for the sweeping lines of new frocks and two-piece ensembles. It's printed in ten different flower designs and each of these is in many beautiful colourings on various grounds of leaf, saxe, powder blue, tango, poppy, lido, navy, nigger, white or black. 36″ wide.' At 6/11d (35 pence) a yard it was certainly a more economical proposition than the same firm's pure silk crêpe de Chine prints which sold for 14/9d (73 pence) per yard.

Post-war technological advances in the manufacture and weaving of rayon resulted in a cloth which compared well with silk in its virtues of handle and drape. Advertising campaigns, notably by Courtaulds, Britain's largest rayon producer, together with luscious new textures and designs, helped to dispel the bad image of 'artificial silk'. No longer was it likely to be highly inflammable, or liable to decompose in a rain storm. Neither did it invariably have a gleaming surface, deemed by many to be vulgar. Delustred finishes, improved resistance to creasing and guaranteed 'Anti Shrink' washability aided rayon's growing popularity.

A rash of trade names appeared to announce the new fabrics. Marshalls produced 'Martialine', 'Crêpe Marelma' and 'Martialesse' besides the widely promoted 'Crêpe Santos'. Their advertisements, recommending the use of

Vogue paper dress patterns, promised that the 'soft clinging quality of this delightful material' would enhance the graceful lines of a slender frock. Tootal Broadhurst Lee Co. Ltd, another Manchester firm, proudly advertised cotton and rayon mixtures alongside their printed rayon taffetas, chiffons and georgettes; 'Tootress ... Smooth, foulardtype fabric', Tootama ... True crepedechine weave', 'Lova ... Soft, resembling lightweight wool' and 'Lystav...Tailors like linen. Supple as silk'.

Crinkled textured crêpes, soft to the touch and brilliantly reflective of printed colours, were especially in demand. They were deemed suitable attire for almost every occasion: frocks for luncheon and bridge parties, garden parties and golf club suppers; frocks for summer afternoons, informal dinner dances, cocktails, an excursion to a restaurant or to the cinema; graceful frocks in which to remain 'cool and smart looking through a London July'. Light to medium weight and sheer fabrics were available for summer wear, and heavier weights for winter dresses.

Fashion journalists extolled the indispensability of crêpe at every opportunity. 'CREPE DE CHINE seems to lose none of its charm for the well dressed woman, and the latest silks of this persuasion are mostly patterned with small designs, either in single flower heads or in little detached bunches of tiny blooms, as though they had been showered lightly over the surface of the material at regular intervals. For afternoon wear these printed crêpe de Chines have never been more popular than they are at present...' reported Kathleen M. Barrow in *Country Life*, April 15 1933. *Harper's Bazaar*, July 1937, decreed '...strawberry pink and black flowered crêpe de Chine for the afternoon frock that is the smart standby of everyone's summer wardrobe.'

The use of floral decoration on cloth was hardly new but the flowers of the 1930s blossomed with fresh life and vigour. Detailed, naturalistic representations in the traditional manner were eschewed in favour of a freedom of line and form closely allied to contemporary movements in the fine and graphic arts. Deceptively casual pen and brush marks combined with tonal

washes skim effortlessly across the surface of a semi-transparent georgette *(plate 9)*, and sketchily outlined patches of colour, suggesting full-blown flower heads, are juxtaposed with roughly cross-hatched leaves *(plate 10)*. Exquisite, hand-painted water-colour effects were ingeniously transferred onto cloth by the specialized 'Galvano' roller printing machines favoured by Continental manufacturers. Bianchini Férier, a leading French producer of luxury materials, used the technique for their brilliant tulips on lustrous satin *(plate 3)*, while F. Ducharne's wrinkled seersucker *(plate 28)* is boldly splashed with loosely drawn blossoms by the same method.

Printing is the cheapest and most versatile method of patterning fabric. The majority of 1930s dress materials were printed by engraved metal roller machines capable of producing vast yardages at competitive prices. Screen-printing, still in its infancy, and block-printing were better suited to short runs of exclusive furnishing fabrics.

Colourings ranged from the restrained harmonies of blue, navy and white harebells and cornflowers on palest beige *(plate 14)*, to riotous galaxies of colour including exotic flora in vivid pinks, mauves, yellows and burnt orange *(plate 23)*. Few designs exceed four to five colours as the cost of engraving rollers at £50 to £300 each (one roller was needed for each colour) made an excessive number of hues prohibitively expensive. A limited palette was not necessarily a disadvantage and the classic combinations of black or navy with white appeared regularly every season. The effectiveness of two and three colour prints is demonstrated by sophisticated French crêpe de Chines: pink edged dianthus on brown *(plate 1)* and white sprays touched with grey green and coral red on black *(plate 21)*. Added variety was occasionally given by the use of opaque dyestuffs; chalky, matt white contrasts subtly against the luminosity of unprinted silk on the petals of lilies and daisies *(plates 11 and 24)*, while gold highlights cascading leaves on a Calico Printers' Association rayon crêpe *(plate 18)*.

In order to combat the plagiarism which has always been rife in the fashion world, fabric designs can be registered under a government protection scheme. The Design Registry, established in 1842 specifically to benefit the textile industry, offers protection for up to fifteen years (an initial five year term, extendable for two further five year periods). Only novel, original designs are eligible and manufacturers must submit samples of cloth showing one whole repeat of the pattern. The Registry diligently carries out searches to ensure that each new application is not identical to, nor closely resembles, any existing Registered Design which is still protected and in copyright. In the mid-1930s an average of twelve thousand textile articles (which included dress fabrics) were registered each year, and many of the materials illustrated here are duplicate samples from the Design Registry's Manchester office. Since the decline of British textile production, the Registry today operates solely from London (as part of the Patents Office) and covers a wide range of manufactured goods.

Tootal Broadhurst Lee Co. Ltd and the Calico Printers' Association (an amalgamation of printworks and merchant businesses) both registered numerous designs throughout the 1930s. Foreign manufacturers with sales outlets in the United Kingdom could also register their works, and two prestigious Lyon firms, Bianchini Férier and F. Ducharne, took advantage of this opportunity on many occasions.

British textile businesses suffered from foreign competition both at home and abroad, and they complained with justification that the British government did not provide as much trade protection as did the governments of, for example, Germany, Italy, Belgium, Holland and France. In addition, foreign goods, particularly French dress fabrics, had a certain glamour and *cachet* attached to them which made them somehow more desirable. It was a widely held belief that all the best dressed women went to Paris for their clothes. This 'snobbishness' was deplored by Ernest Goodale (of Warner & Sons Ltd) in an address to the Royal Society of

Arts at the end of the decade, and he surprised many of his audience by revealing that 'British manufacturers of dress materials who were unable to sell them to buyers in this country, frequently sold them to wholesale houses in Paris. British buyers, on visiting that city, quite unknowingly bought these British fabrics in the firm belief that they were the latest products of French looms.'

Although many thousands of garments were made from the millions of yards of flower strewn materials, surprisingly few 1930s floral patterned dresses survive in museum collections. This selection of textile samples from the Victoria and Albert Museum can only hint at the colour, richness and gaiety that these frocks must have provided in the harsh economic climate of these years. The outbreak of war in 1939 altered life irrevocably. Non-essential manufacture was curtailed, raw materials were no longer readily available and textile factories became producers of goods, such as blackout cloth and parachute silk, for the war effort. Women found more urgent activities than tea parties and bridge games and, of necessity, ultra feminine frocks were replaced by plainer utilitarian garments.

All works illustrated are printed dress fabrics from the Department of Textile Furnishings and Dress, Victoria and Albert Museum. Photography by Daniel McGrath.

1. Crêpe de Chine, *Bianchini Férier, French, 1935*. 2. Silk crêpe, *Bianchini Férier, French, 1935*. 3. Silk satin, *Bianchini Férier, French, 1936*. 4. Rayon crêpe, *Calico Printers' Association, British, 1935*. 5. Rayon georgette, *Calico Printers' Association, British, 1933*. 6. Cotton, *D. Marshall & Co. Ltd, British, c. 1933*. 7. Cotton voile, *Calico Printers' Association, British, 1930*. 8. Rayon crêpe, *Calico Printers' Association, British, 1935*. 9. Rayon georgette, *possibly Tootal Broadhurst Lee Co. Ltd, British, mid 1930s*. 10. Rayon georgette, *Calico Printers' Association, British, 1932*. 11. Silk crêpe, *F. Ducharne, French, 1937*. 12. Silk crêpe, *Bianchini Férier, French, 1935*. 13. Rayon georgette, *Tootal Broadhurst Lee Co. Ltd, British, 1934*. 14. Silk crêpe, *Bianchini Férier, French, 1935*. 15. Rayon crêpe, *Calico Printers' Association, British, 1935*. 16. Rayon crêpe, *Calico Printers' Association, British, 1935*. 17. Rayon georgette, *Tootal Broadhurst Lee Co. Ltd, British, 1934*. 18. Rayon crêpe, *Calico Printers' Association, British, 1937*. 19. Rayon crêpe, *Calico Printers' Association, British, 1935*. 20. Fancy rayon crêpe, *Calico Printers' Association, British, 1935*. 21. Crêpe de Chine, *Bianchini Férier, French, 1934*. 22. Rayon crêpe, *Calico Printers' Association, British, 1935*. 23. Silk and rayon satin, *probably French, c. 1937*. 24. Silk crêpe, *F. Ducharne, French, 1936*. 25. Crêpe de Chine, *Bianchini Férier, French, 1935*. 26. Fancy weave glazed cotton, *F. Ducharne, French, 1936*. 27. Silk marocain, *F. Ducharne, French, 1935*. 28. Silk seersucker, *F. Ducharne, French, 1936*. 29. Figured silk, *Stehli Silks Corporation, American, 1930*. 30. Silk crêpe, *Calico Printers' Association, British, 1936*. 31. Silk seersucker, *F. Ducharne, French, 1935*. 32. Silk seersucker, *F. Ducharne, French, 1935*.

Plates 1-5, 7, 8, 10-22, 24-28 and 30-32 given by the Manchester Design Registry. Plate 6 given by the British Institute of Industrial Art. Plate 29 given by the Stehli Silks Corporation.

THE PLATES

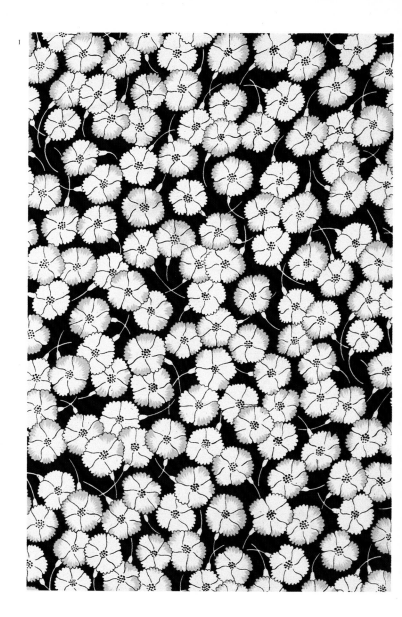

13

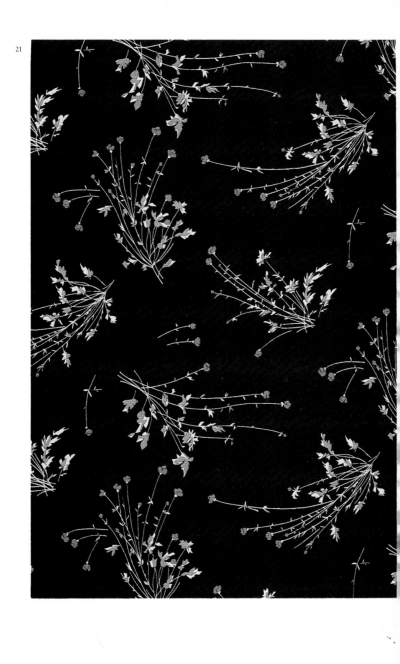

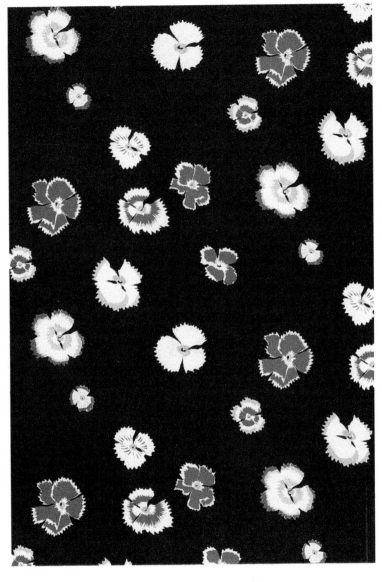

358697

THE
VICTORIA
& ALBERT
COLOUR
BOOKS